# our story

# our story

## by john dingwall

### additional interview material by julie maccaskill

BOXTREE

First published in 1998 by Boxtree, an imprint of Macmillan Publishers Ltd,
25 Eccleston Place, London, SW1W 9NF and Basingstoke

Associated companies throughout the world

ISBN 0 7522 1191 9

Copyright © 1998 911. Licensed by $i/s$ Another BIG product.

The right of John Dingwall to be identified as the author of this work has been asserted
by him in accordance with the Copyright, Designs and Patents Act 1988.

9 8 7 6 5 4 3 2 1

A CIP catalogue record for this book is available from the British Library

Typeset & designed by Blackjacks, London
Reproduction by Scanners
Printed in Italy by New Interlitho S.p.A. - Milan

# contents

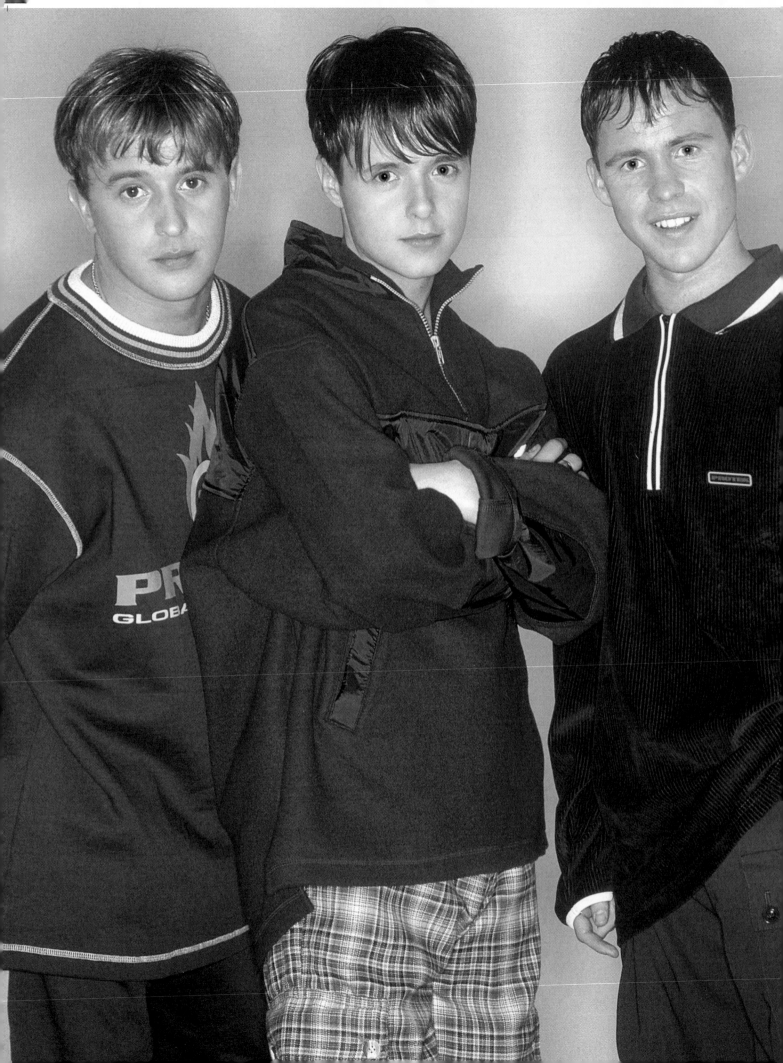

# introduction

When three boys from the North of England chose to move to Scotland in their bid for pop stardom, many in the pop industry thought they were crazy.

But the gamble soon paid the sort of dividends which had Britain's most successful music moguls questioning their own A&R (artists and repertoire) policies, expensive marketing strategies and complex flow charts as they sat in their high-tech London offices. How was it that three penniless young men could twice gatecrash their way into the charts on a shoestring budget?

In the early days, Jimmy Constable, Lee Brennan and Spike Dawbarn – collectively known as 911 after the US emergency services' phone number – had been turned down each time they drove down to London to knock on doors in search of a record deal.

But the boys were determined not to be downhearted.

Their début single, a cover of the 80s funk-soul band Shalamar's 'Night To Remember', had been released on the Scottish independent label, the Ginga Recording Co., but its success was considered a fluke by the big boys when the song charted at number thirty-eight in the UK top forty in May 1996.

So it wasn't until their second single 'Love Sensation' stormed all the way to number twenty-one, just two months later, that the pop industry finally sat up and took notice of 911 and the Backlash team who were behind them.

If 911 could repeatedly have hit records, what would be the rewards for the major label which decided to put its might behind three handsome young men, already on their way to becoming one of Britain's favourite bands?

Had the record company bigwigs looked closer, they would have found that there was nothing simple about the route that Lee, Jimmy and Spike had taken to the top of the charts. Their short-term success was fuelled by the same ingredients which have seen 911, in the space of two years, become favourites with over a million fans worldwide. Their story is one of a remarkable rise to fame, fraught with adversity, and one which serves to highlight the good-natured grit and determination of three talented down-to-earth lads who held on to their childhood dreams of pop stardom.

Now, after six consecutive chart hits from their début album, 'The Journey', which went silver within a week of its release, and over a million sales around the world, the 911 story can be told in full for the first time.

# lee

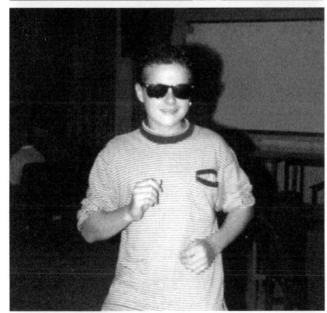

Born 27 September 1975 at Carlisle's City Maternity Hospital, Lee Anthony Brennan grew up as one of five children in his hometown.

In his early years, he hoped to emulate Carlisle United strikers Dan O'Riordan and Andy Hill, both of whom had become the top scorers for the club in the mid-1980s. But, despite trials and visits from club scouts, Lee was turned down because, at 'five foot four and three quarters', he was considered too small to pose a threat to the towering defenders who dominate the English football leagues.

Dreaming of being a household name for as long as he can remember, Lee admits: 'I always felt that one day, I'd get on TV, even if it was only for five minutes. When I was younger I went to Bobby Charlton's school of excellence. I loved football. I even captained the county football team under-14s and under-16s and won Player of the Year twice. I wanted to be a footballer when I grew up. I told my careers officer I was going to be famous. Something told me I would do something I would be noticed for. But I failed to make the grade as a professional footballer with Carlisle United, which is my favourite team. Soon after, singing appealed to me.'

It hadn't helped that Lee was an asthma sufferer who had to use his inhaler at half-time.

'Lee always said he was going to be famous,' recalls his mum, Una. 'From nine or ten he would practise signing his autograph. Then he had his heart set on being a footballer.'

Dad, Frances, continues, 'He played in the school and local youth team, and brought home all sorts of

medals and trophies. But, when it came to playing in the big league, they thought he was too small. And when they saw him using his inhaler, Lee's chances of playing serious football games were numbered.'

Despite the disappointment, Lee remains a fan of the club: 'I'm a big Carlisle fan. I've been supporting them since I was seven years old. These days, what with band commitments, I don't get to as many games as I'd like to, but I'm always in touch with what's going on there. However far away I am, I always find out how Carlisle United have done. I still remember playing football at school and dreaming of playing for them, but it wasn't to be.'

Lee's health posed other problems for him in childhood. The fact that the heart-throb singer is able to endure 911's gruelling schedule is even more remarkable when you know that he has twice had to battle against the rare cancer, Hodgkin's Disease – first at eight years old and, again, when the illness recurred as Lee turned thirteen.

'I felt constantly tired,' he says, 'I spent months in hospital. But, throughout, I told myself that, one day, I would be on TV. Even while the doctors and nurses were struggling to save my life, I knew I would be an entertainer.'

Lee's mum used to manage a snooker club in Carlisle and Lee, just twelve, would regularly play there with friend Paul Cowing. His skill on the tables earned him his first television appearance when he and Paul were

spotted by a children's TV researcher who invited the pair to appear with former world snooker champion John Parrott on ITV's Saturday morning programme *Get Fresh*. Both lads were shown a few expert shots by John, before taking part in a general knowledge quiz against each other, which Paul won.

'So then I wanted to be a snooker player,' Lee says. 'I practised every day. Meeting John Parrott was dead cool. But, once I realized I wasn't going to be a famous snooker player, I thought I'd give singing a try.'

At seventeen, Lee began to show musical promise.

'Lee's next goal was to become a singer,' says Una. 'He was still living in Carlisle and I had moved to the North East of England, but I used to go with him to auditions around the Newcastle area. He had a couple with showbands, but he was always too small and looked out of place. At one audition, the band wanted two male singers up front. The other chap was over 6 ft, and he and Lee looked ridiculous side by side!'

# spike

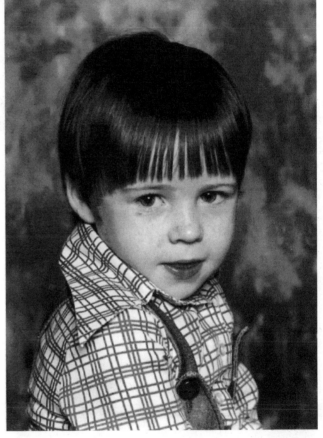

Simon James Dawbarn was born in Warrington, near Manchester, on 5 August 1974, the second of three sons to his parents Mo and Mike. He was nicknamed Spike by his friends because of the spikey haircut he had as a teenager.

'Spike was a very mischievous little boy,' recalls his mum, Mo. 'On one memorable occasion when he was six years old, he was escorted to the door by a 6ft 6in policeman. Spike was less than 3ft tall and had been caught posting dirt through letter-boxes. When the policeman caught him, all he could say was, 'Beam me up, Scotty'!

'Perhaps a sign that he would one day be a pop star was that his favourite programme was, without doubt, *Top of the Pops*,' says dad, Mike. 'From the age of two, he watched it every week and danced along to the music. As he grew, he played music loud all the time and, when he danced along to it, the ceiling lights shook.'

Like Lee, Spike loved football.

'I grew up in a three-bedroomed semi with a garden. I shared a bedroom with my brother Mike and,' Spike laughed, 'we had Manchester United wallpaper with matching lampshades!'

He also showed a drive and determination, possessed by only the choice few of today's potential pop stars.

He worked as a bricklayer on leaving school, but confesses that his ambition was always to dance his way to the top. As he completed a bricklaying course, he told his dad: 'Right. Now that that's over, I'm going to become a dancer.' 'I always wanted to be on stage,' Spike adds. 'Ever since I was little, I've danced.'

Like most teenagers, Spike liked to go clubbing and enjoyed regular trips to Mr Smith's in Warrington where he was soon spotted by Clive, a charismatic head dancer there.

Clive recognized a raw energy and talent in Spike and was soon showing him moves which would lead Spike, unwittingly, into his first job as an entertainer – as a dancer for the 1980s cult late-night Granada TV show *The Hit Man & Her*.

# jïmmy

Liverpool-born Jimmy Constable arrived shortly before 10 a.m., on 21 September 1973, at the city's Oxford Street Maternity Hospital.

His mum, Margaret, and dad, Ronnie, had been kept up most of the night waiting for their only son and have remained a constant encouragement throughout all the time he was seeking his true vocation.

'We took him to see Shakin' Stevens when he was ten years old, and he met him backstage after the concert and became a big fan after that,' recalls his dad.

Jimmy's mum remembers only too well her son's earliest pop efforts as a juvenile Shakin' Stevens impersonator.

'He was into Shakin' Stevens and modelled himself on him from a very early age,' she says. 'He sang, danced, everything. There were posters on the walls. Whatever Shaky

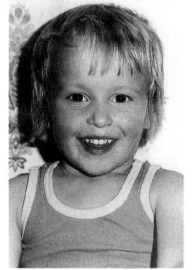

did, Jimmy did. At his eleventh birthday party, he and all his mates dressed up as Shakin' Stevens. Jimmy's always been musical.'

'Shakin' Stevens,' Jimmy admits, 'was my favourite pop star when I was young. I even won a talent competition dressed as him. To this day, the lads still give me a hard time for this, but they're just jealous because they can't sing "Green Door" as well as I can!'

Jimmy's mum, dad and little sister, Nicola, moved to Runcorn in the north-west of Liverpool. When Jimmy was seventeen, his dad found him a job as an apprentice mechanic with Kwik Fit. At that time, Jimmy wanted to be a policeman and while working towards that goal he worked for a while as a lifeguard in a leisure club in Runcorn.

'I wanted to be anything that anyone would let me have as a career!' Jimmy jokes. 'I didn't have much in the way of ambition – one minute I wanted to be a policeman and then I became a lifeguard because I was presented with the opportunity. As a lifeguard, I never did very much. I always missed work but I looked the part in the shorts!'

He excelled at sports in school and fantasized about making the legendary first team at Liverpool FC. But his hopes of playing for Liverpool were shattered when he failed a trial with the Mersey club. Instead Wrexham took him on, though he spent little of his time between the goal posts.

'I told my careers teacher I wanted to be an engineer,' Jimmy recalls, 'so I tried that for a while. I did a six-month apprenticeship at Wrexham Football Club where I got to polish the stars' boots. Well, the nearest thing they had to stars at Wrexham!'

When Jimmy was in his teens, his parents separated and he soon saw the entertainment world as a way to do something positive with his life.

'When my parents split,' he said, 'it was quite hard on my sister Nicola, but I think I coped slightly better because I was more independent than her. I'd left home before they split up and had come to terms with life without them being together. It was a very hard time for everybody, but you've got to believe that you're not on your own and that there are people who can help you through your hard times. I had a good upbringing from my parents but I rebelled slightly when I got older. A lot of kids do. When you're younger, you don't always think about the consequences of your actions. It's really difficult being a teenager. You've got so much going on in your life and, at the same time, you're trying to figure out who you are. As time goes on, it doesn't actually stop being difficult – you just cope better.'

Like Spike, Jimmy's big break came when he met Clive at Mr Smith's and began work there as a dancer.

He had seen Spike at the nightclub and was quickly introduced to him. Needless to say, the pair hit it off straight away and they doubled up to train for strenuous dance routines.

Before long, Spike and Jimmy were chosen to perform together on the late-night ITV show *The Hit Man & Her*.

A product of the 1980s, the programme was made up almost entirely of live footage at clubs all over the UK and was shown way past most sensible people's bedtime. It was co-presented by Michaela Strachan and record producer Pete Waterman – one third of the production team known as PWL which had helped launch the careers of acts such as Kylie Minogue and Rick Astley, and dominated the singles charts in the late 1980s.

Jimmy knew that working on the *Hit Man & Her* show was his big chance. If he could impress people with his dance routines, who knew where it would lead?

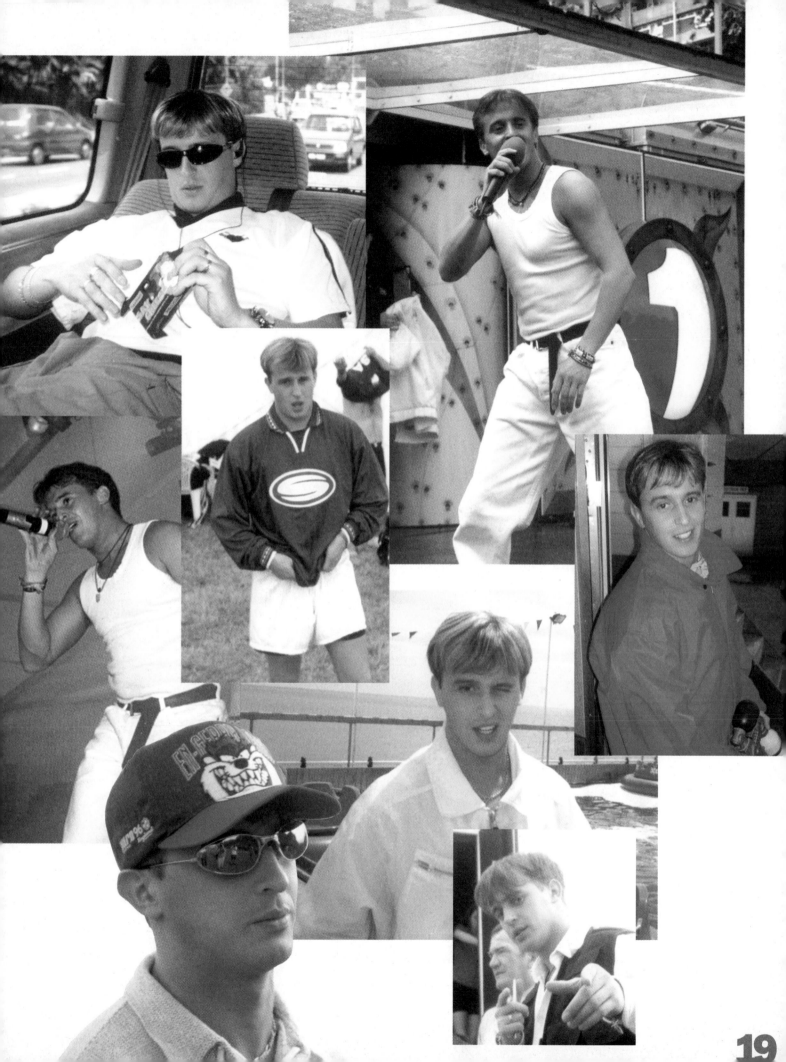

# the beginning

Spike also knew that working on *The Hit Man and Her* was an opportunity of a lifetime and that he would have to graft if he was to fill the shoes of his predecessor, a chap called Jason Orange who had quit the programme to try his hand at pop music in a band called Take That.

In fact, long before they formed the group, each of the lads in 911 knew the meaning of hard work.

Spike was a paper-boy as a lad, delivering the *Manchester Evening News* for two years. Little did he realize then that he was spending his earnings on market research for the pop career which lay ahead of him.

'I was about fourteen when I did the paper run so that I could earn some extra money,' Spike recalls. 'I spent the cash on hip hop records so I suppose that was market research! And I bought some new clothes. I used to get up at the crack of dawn and even worked after school. It's really funny to think I'm now appearing in the paper rather than delivering it.'

Lee, too, quickly got a taste of things to come. Within two weeks of leaving school, he started a job with the sign-writing company which produced and designed the Eddie Stobart livery for the company's fleet of trucks.

'I got to put the names of all these different companies on the side of the trucks,' Lee recalls. 'At the time it was hard work – each one had to be perfect. Occasionally, we had to work through the night on new trucks, but I enjoyed it.'

It wasn't long, though, before Lee moved on to work at a ten-pin bowling alley where his job was, among other things, to clean the bowling balls. 'It was the highlight of my week,' he jokes.

There, Lee was surprised to find an unofficial Lee Brennan fan club quickly growing around him, filled with adoring female members who would chase him for autographs. The young women swooned over his boyish good looks and asked if they could take his photograph. 'Can I take my friend's picture standing next to you, then, can she take mine?' they would ask.

'Even before I was in 911,' Lee says, 'I was being treated like somebody special. It was strange and made me think about the future. I dreamed of being in a band.'

But Lee didn't just dream of fame. He took positive action. He tried to make it on to the telly by turning up at local auditions for ITV's *Stars In Your Eyes* impersonating Wet Wet Wet singer Marti Pellow. He made it to the shortlist of 300 but failed his final audition when the pressure got to him and he forgot the words to 'Goodnight Girl'.

'I made a pretty bad Marti Pellow, actually, but I was so desperate to find fame that I thought I'd give it a go on *Stars In Your Eyes*,' Lee admits. 'It was a disaster. I couldn't believe that I could forget the words to "Goodnight Girl". Worst of all, the winner of that year's final was a Marti Pellow impersonator!

Meanwhile, as a result of their energetic and fun dance routines, Spike and Jimmy were already developing their own fans even before 911 was formed. They were often asked to dance at roadshows starring other boy bands, and the *Hit Man & Her* show provided the ideal platform for them to test their latest moves on a responsive and, often, adoring audience.

'When we were on the show we were getting better responses than the acts we were supporting, so it seemed the natural thing to form a group of our own,' says Jimmy.

The one thing they needed more than anything else, they figured, was a manager.

Although Steve Gilmour's music biz credentials were still at a formative stage, those who met this hungry young entrepreneur were impressed by his enthusiasm and determination. Steve had worked nights as a DJ, and had spent a short time at BBC Radio Scotland researching for their magazine programmes *Earshot* and *Bite The Wax*.

But, perhaps most importantly, Steve had been an agent for promotional tours by teen acts, including PJ and Duncan and Boyzone, as well as legendary entertainers Rolf Harris and Norman Wisdom.

Spike and Jimmy first met Steve at a show he had co-promoted with Carlisle's radio station CFM in March 1995. They had been booked as a warm-up act for the pop band Worlds Apart, who were the main attraction that night. As Steve watched Spike and Jimmy's routine, he noticed the extremely positive reaction from the crowd.

'Girls in the crowd were going wild for them,' says Steve. 'After that, I would look out for them at roadshows. Each time I met them I saw that more and more people were following these two guys who were, at that stage, only dancers. I could see, even then, that they were special. We got on well immediately and they told me they wanted to form a band.'

Just a couple of months after their first meeting, Jimmy and Spike asked him to manage them. At first Steve turned them down flat.

'I had never thought of managing a band,' Steve admits. 'I was very honest with them and told them I didn't know the first thing about management. I recognised the fact that, at the end of the day, a manager is someone who is responsible for an artist's career. Back then I wasn't willing to take on that level of responsibility. But they were persistent. As time went on, more and more fans started following them. Jimmy and Spike were more hungry for success than ever – they really wanted to start a band of their own. Wherever they went, the guys were mobbed by fans and they kept asking me to manage them.'

Every time their paths crossed, Jimmy would show Steve the sacks of fan-mail they were receiving after each roadshow date and, two months later, Jimmy and Spike were one of seven acts booked at the Sands Centre in Carlisle, again for CFM.

Over the months, Steve had become convinced of Spike and Jimmy's future as pop stars and it was at this roadshow that he decided that the time was now right to manage them.

But, while Steve had been impressed by Spike and Jimmy's professionalism, his experience as an agent told him that Spike and Jimmy were short of one crucial ingredient – a singer.

By chance, Lee had been persuaded to take his little sister, Becky, backstage to meet Spike and Jimmy at a show in November '95.

'Becky fancied Spike,' recalls Lee, 'and I had to introduce her to him. But I hit it off with the guys straight away. They told me they were looking for a singer and I told them I wanted to start a singing career. We laughed about the coincidence but the timing couldn't have been better. The first meeting was very relaxed and it wasn't long after that that Spike and Jimmy got in touch to say they wanted to see me about being in their band. They wanted me to audition for them.'

The following week Spike and Jimmy travelled to Carlisle where Lee had booked a rehearsal room in a dance studio. Having done his best to impress Spike and

RAY BURMISTON

Jimmy, Lee waited while the guys stepped outside to talk over what they had seen so far of the budding member of their as yet un-named group.

It was Spike who pushed things forward. 'He can dance,' he told Jimmy. 'He's got it.'

Soon after, a second audition in Glasgow also went well. But it wasn't until another visit to Glasgow that Spike, Jimmy and their manager Steve were a hundred per cent convinced that Lee should join the band.

Geographically, this posed a problem. While Steve was based in Glasgow, Lee lived in Carlisle, Spike in Warrington and Jimmy in Liverpool. If they were going to be able to rehearse and perform all the functions required of future superstars, something had to be done.

The solution was simple – they moved into Steve's three-bedroomed flat in Glasgow's south side.

Within days, Jimmy and Spike discovered that Lee had been economical with the truth in order to join the band. Eager to become a singer and impress on them his fitness, Lee had told the boys that he jogged several miles every morning. But when they took him for a leisurely jog through the local park, Lee gave up, exhausted. But Lee needn't have worried about being found out. Both his partners just laughed.

'It was so funny watching Lee struggle to keep up with us,' Spike remembers. 'We just laughed and decided to let him stay anyway.'

Jimmy, Lee and Spike, knowing that first impressions tend to last, were only too aware that the trio's first official public outing, in May 1995, was all important. It was a Friday night, just two days before their official launch as a band.

Looking back, the manager at Bonkers Show Bar, in Glasgow's Hope Street, got a great deal. He agreed to allow the boys to sing one song – 'Night To Remember' – for no fee.

Jimmy, Lee and Spike used this experience to give them the confidence to perform a second show the following morning. This time, The Bankrupt Clothing Store in Glasgow became the unusual venue.

Bankrupt had been running a series of adverts over a two-week spell on Clyde One FM and had tagged 911's scheduled appearance on to the end of their sales' pitch. Naturally, a free concert proved immensely popular with the fans. But the store had underestimated 911's popularity.

As the crowd packed the store, with others spilling out on to the pedestrianized street, fans chanted 911's name throughout the live appearance.

That Sunday, the band returned to Carlisle's Pagoda Nightclub for the official launch of 911, co-promoted by CFM Radio. A £2 admission fee paid for the sound system and lights in return for a three-song show by 911.

A TV camera crew from BBC Scotland and three newspapers were there to report on the band, already being tipped for greater things.

Later, the group used the media coverage to help win some coveted spots on roadshows throughout the UK.

'When we started out, we went to every gig going to get ourselves known but we didn't get paid,' explains Spike. 'We lived with our manager and he paid for every-

thing and gave us about £20 pocket money each a week. We get a bit more than that now!'

Jimmy, ever the realist, looked on their humble beginnings as a challenge. 'Before getting into something like this, you have to know why you want to do it. It's about performing, not the money. Money is just a bonus.

In the early days 911's determination to succeed was coupled only with their desire to get out there and meet their fans and so it followed that a gruelling touring schedule would be required if they were to achieve their ambitions. At times the touring seemed never ending... and there were some bizarre shows along the way. One of their oddest audiences turned out in Penrith, Cumbria.

'There were about twenty people there – all farmers with their wives on a night out,' a bemused Lee told Smash Hits. 'They completely ignored us. I think they were more interested in milking their cows.'

Another problem the band faced was finding original songs.

John McLaughlin, a Glaswegian songwriter, saw the band at a roadshow in Glasgow's Scottish Exhibition and Conference Centre.

'They had blagged on to a spot on the Radio 1 Roadshow which was part of that year's Clothes Show event,' says John, who was immediately impressed by the three guys on stage. 'As soon as I saw them I realized they had something special. They covered a Bobby Brown song "Every Little Step" and I thought there was a special ingredient that had been missing from other acts that day.'

John wondered if they had a manager and was quickly introduced to Steve Gilmour.

'Steve, myself and the boys clicked straight away,' John recalls. 'We all got on great.'

That night, John went back to his home studio buzzing with ideas and co-wrote 'Can't Stop' with fellow songwriter, Gordon Goudie.

When 911 heard the demo version of the song the following morning, they were so impressed they immediately decided to include it in their live show. The song would later make it on to the band's début album, 'The Journey' which would be released some twelve months later.

But Jimmy, Lee and Spike also wanted something raunchy to help set their stage performances alive. Could John and Gordon come up with the goods by delivering something raunchy?, they asked.

A day later John and Gordon delivered a song called 'Bodyshakin''.

Impressed, the boys asked them to come up with an out-and-out pop song, and were stunned when they penned 'Love Sensation', the next day.

Another day passed, and, this time, 'Don't Make Me Wait' was completed with the help of former Associates' rocker, Alan Rankin, who was working as a music business lecturer at a local college.

Jimmy, Spike and Lee listened to the four-track demo, amazed at what they were hearing.

But John and Gordon were slower when it came to another future album track, 'One More Try'. It took a whole week!

'In the space of just over a week, we had recorded demos of all those tracks,' laughs John.

'So many people put you down in the music business,' Jimmy reveals. 'You have to be positive, and the only way to stay positive is to have people around you who are also positive. We're very fortunate in that we have a great team of people around us who really believe in what we're doing – we're all passionate about 911.'

Lee continues, 'By remaining positive you can deal with any situation, however impossible it may seem. For us every step of our career has been a challenge and we've always managed to find a way round them. At the beginning, we could have just given up hope. We'd been turned down by every major record company. We'd sent off demos and had done loads of London showcases. But no matter how hard we tried we just kept on getting knockbacks from A&R men at record companies. We had no experience in making our own records, but that didn't stop us from going for it. That's what I mean about being positive. Some people might have lost hope and given up. But we decided we would learn as we go along. We already knew we had a Scottish fan base which was the envy of many groups who were already successful. We knew we would succeed.'

In order to succeed, Steve knew that, in much the same way as 911 had needed a third member to become a group, he would also have to build a team of people to give 911 the chance to be as successful as they deserved.

Martin Wright met Steve when he was working at BBC Scotland on a radio training course. Steve needed someone to create a database to keep a record of 911's increasing fan base and Martin was experienced in computer programming. Martin came on board to do one week's work. Two years later he's still there and now he manages the hugely successful 911 Official Fan Club, which boasts over 55,000 members worldwide and recently won the best fan club award as voted by viewers of Teletext.

Stuart Owen was working with the MIST (Music in Scotland Trust) across the corridor from Steve's office. He liked the set up and saw a future in 911. In the early days Stuart toured with the band, taking them from one PA to another and to roadshows all over the country. He is now the production co-ordinator for 911 and is currently working on their first UK tour.

Press and PR Manager Julie MacCaskill was working as a music promoter with the Glasgow-based festival The 10-Day Weekend when her path crossed with 911's. She put the unsigned band on as part of the final showcase in Glasgow's George Square which was later to become a testament to 911's popularity. Steve needed a press manager to promote his new band and Julie was impressed with what she saw. Julie recalls, 'There was something about them, they were magnificent stage performers even in the early days. Working with them was a challenge and I felt sure that they had a big future ahead of them.'

Stringent self-taught businessman Frank Shapiro who had a passion for music was so impressed by 911 and the team behind them that he was eager to get involved early on. He saw the future in 911 and recognised the determination and passion in the team surrounding them. Steve had the creative experience with some business knowledge and Frank brought extensive business experience and some creative input. They joined forces and together they steered Backlash, the company behind 911, into a new phase. By February 1996, the core team were together and work on building 911 into pop superstars could now begin.

From the very beginning, Lee, Spike and Jimmy recognised the importance of their fans. Nowadays, the group has learnt to come to terms with the lengths that fans will go to when trying to meet the group.

'One girl,' Jimmy laughs, 'pretended to be my cousin. She came into our hotel and asked for my room number. Reception rang me up and said: "Your cousin's downstairs". But when I went down there were a load of fans there. I had to speak to reception and straighten things out. When things like this happen, we don't get mad at the fans. They're just trying to get close to you. We get shocking letters from them. I think we must have some

of the rudest letters around. And some of the banners we get. Honestly!'

Back in February 1996, rumours had reached the 911 offices which, if true, would change the face of British pop music overnight. The 911 boys and their management team huddled in their tiny office listening to Radio 1 to find out if it was true that Take That were splitting up. The confirmation came when Gary Barlow announced: 'The rumours are true. After today, Take That will be no more.'

Lee, a huge fan of Take That, was too shell-shocked to speak. 'We were absolutely gutted,' he recalls. 'Take That had made such a big impact on my career choice. They were so professional, true performers.'

A month later, in March, 911 had won GMTV's *Search for the Next Big Thing*, by a staggering 10,000 phone-in votes against Crush, Ivor Mathias and the Super Furry Animals.

'It was fantastic winning,' Jimmy remembers. 'My mum's so proud she's started showing off my baby photos to friends.'

To this day, that significant first award still has pride of place in the Backlash offices.

But not everybody appreciated 911's growing popularity. Days after winning the award the guys were forced to move out of the flat they shared by disgruntled neighbours. Was it the dance routines practised on bare floorboards or the fans outside chanting for the band at all hours which upset them so much?

The final straw seemed to come when more than fifty girls finally succeeded in locating the 911 flat in the south side of Glasgow.

'We used to live together,' explains Lee, 'but our neighbours got sick of the fans outside and threatened us because we caused so much disruption... so we had to move.'

The Backlash team were now working closely with their three-man songwriting team, John McLaughlin, Gordon Goudie and Alan Rankin – all of whom had a perfect music pedigree for helping to craft hit songs for 911.

Meanwhile, if the boys had lacked any confidence about making the transition from dancers to full-time singers, that was soon taken care of by their Glaswegian singing tutor Deirdre Turnbull. Rather than simply teaching them how to sing, Deirdre gave them valuable lessons on how to avoid straining their vocal chords.

Throughout the first year, the band's shows and press and media coverage had helped them compile a database of over 5000 fans. The group also kept in constant contact with record companies in the hope of snapping up a deal which would enable them to release their first single.

Eventually, reckons Spike, it reached make or break time.

'We knew we had to put a record out otherwise our fans would lose interest,' he says. 'We needed a record deal.'

Jimmy continues, 'We got standard rejection letters from record companies A&R departments stating that our material was unsuitable. But we decided that we weren't going to give up – we knew that one day these record companies would regret saying no to 911.'

Independent record companies were approached to produce and distribute 911's first single. One label agreed to re-mix the band's demo version 'Night To Remember' but refused to splash out on a new recording of the song.

When the results of the re-mix were played back to Jimmy, Spike, Lee and the Backlash team, there was an embarrassed silence.

'It was a techno version of 911,' explains Jimmy. 'After hearing it we were all on a big downer.'

Steve took action. 'I called the label and told them the mix wasn't liked by any of us. But they wouldn't budge and insisted it should be our first single. Then they hung up on us. We were back at square one.'

The whole team sat down in complete disbelief. What would they do now? They began talking about how they could get round this impossible situation and after some discussion it was decided that the team should put out 911's début single themselves. And so the Ginga Recording Company was born.

'There's nobody who believes in this like we do. Let's do it ourselves,' said an optimistic Jimmy.

Looking back, the band sees that moment as the turning point in their career.

'Everybody shook hands,' recalls Lee. 'When we think back to that one day, we know it was the day that we realized we could go out on our own and put our first record out ourselves. No matter what anyone else thought, we could carry on and make a success of it.'

RAY BURMISTON

# 'night to remember'

Just days earlier, Jamie Nelson, a respected A&R man with Parlophone Records, had recommended that the band approach Eliot Kennedy, a top record producer, in a bid to get him to record with them.

'Eliot's a really nice guy,' he told the team. 'Give him a call. He might just go for it.'

Eliot Kennedy, one of the industry's most respected songwriters and producers, already had an impressive CV of acts he had worked miracles with, including revamping Scots singer Lulu's career with the song 'Independence'. He had also produced several songs on Take That's 'Everything Changes' album including the title track sung by Robbie Williams which had topped the charts some months before. Jimmy, Lee and Spike were keen to enlist his services as the band's producer.

'Our manager sent him a demo tape, a live video, some press cuttings and a couple of photographs,' says Spike. ' Thankfully, it got his interest.'

The day after the band had contacted the producer, Eliot Kennedy called to say he had heard about the group and would watch the video later that week. A couple of days later, the band got the call they had hoped for. A meeting was set. 911 and Steve agreed to go to Eliot's home studio, located at the rear of a discreet three-bedroomed semi-detached house near Nottinghamshire's Sherwood Forest. Once there, they talked about the songs Eliot had written, others he had produced, and why they wanted him to come on board with 911.

'Basically, we like your style,' Jimmy told him.

During the meeting, Eliot then played the boys a song that he had just written with an unknown group called The Spice Girls. The track was called 'Say You'll Be There'. At the time, Victoria Adams, Geri Halliwell, Emma Bunton, Melanie Chisolm and Melanie Brown had yet to release their first single 'Wannabe' which would shoot the band to number one in the UK. In fact Posh, Ginger, Baby, Scary and Sporty weren't sure if they wanted to record and release 'Say You'll Be There' as a single or track on their planned debut album and that left Eliot able to offer the track to 911.

'This is an available song,' Eliot told the boys. 'Are you interested in using it?'

The guys knew the chart potential of 'Say You'll Be There' as soon as they heard it, and couldn't believe that Eliot was offering it to them.

'This is a hit record,' said an excited Lee.

'Well, why don't we do it?' came Eliot's calm response.

He gave them a cassette copy of the song to take away with them and soon 911 were preparing to record the song with Eliot.

'The next phone call I received was from the girls' manager to say, "Sorry, but we're cutting it," says Eliot. 'They had decided it was going to be a Spice Girls' single and that was that. The Spice Girls took priority because they had co-written it. But there was no bad feeling from 911 because it led to us working together on a whole load of other songs.'

As Jimmy, Lee and Spike headed south to record with Eliot, a chance meeting with Take That's Howard

Donald at a service station provided them with good wishes for the trip and some prophetic words of advice.

Howard had worked with Eliot and considered him a close friend.

'Enjoy this moment,' the dreadlocked star told the boys. 'There'll be a time when you'll think you're never going to make it. Then, overnight, everything will change and you'll want to go back to the way you were and wonder what it was like when you used to do personal appearances. But you won't be able to. You'll think, what happened? Enjoy this moment, because it's fantastic and it'll be over all too soon.'

Just then, a chap approached them and said to Howard: 'My girlfriend really likes you. Can I have your autograph?'

As Howard scribbled his name, he said to the guy: 'No problem. But you'd better get these guys, too, because they're going to be huge.'

'It was very weird meeting Howard,' Lee laughs. 'I've watched him perform in front of thousands of people on video and there he was standing talking to us. He was a very down-to-earth guy and dead nice.'

'It was cool meeting a superstar,' adds Spike. 'I just couldn't believe how normal he was.'

When 911 returned to Eliot's home, it was to record the vocals for 'Night To Remember'. Eliot had already recorded the backing track which they loved. He sat down with Jimmy, Spike and Lee to discuss the direction they wanted their music to take. 911 and their team were very sure of where they saw 911 in the pop music picture.

'We had to work on the direction because I saw no point in going over the same ground that I had covered with Take That,' says Eliot. 'It was good because the guys were into things like R&B and funk and had plenty of good ideas about what they wanted to do with their careers.'

The boys couldn't wait to get started and, for the next three days, stayed over at the studio, which was part of Eliot's home.

The rap for the song was written by the renowned producer and Jimmy on the first day while the others popped out to the shops. By the time they got back it was ready to record.

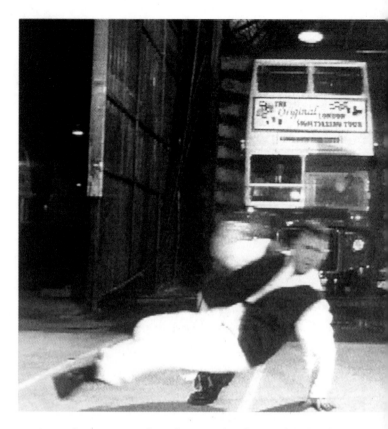

As well as cutting their first single, Jimmy, Lee and Spike endeavoured to beat Eliot at their favourite Playstation games until two in the morning, and could also be found playing football in the nearby park during afternoon breaks to relieve the tension of being in the studio for long periods of time.

'It was less like making a record and more like having a party,' Spike recalls. 'Eliot made it feel like we were staying at his house as friends and doing a bit of recording while we were there. It was a very relaxed atmosphere. Eliot is a brilliant ideas man. He makes the difference between a record sounding good and it coming across as really special. He's got a proven track record of hit-writing and producing, so he was perfect for us. And he's not bad at the Playstation either.'

Despite his lack of experience, Lee had instantly adapted to being a studio vocalist.

On the last night, the boys went to Leeds where they met up with the rest of the Backlash team at a concert and everyone listened to the eagerly-awaited new version of 'Night To Remember'.

'There we were in Leeds after doing a show,' remembers Jimmy. 'We had parked outside a MacDonalds and all piled into the car to listen to the finished track

together. When the song was over we all started cheering and shouting. We had some funny looks from passers-by, I can tell you, but we didn't care.'

As soon as the digital audio tape of the song was copied and sent to Scotland, the team set about getting the single released. Within weeks, 20,000 copies had been pressed on the Ginga Recording Company label.

Meantime, 911 embarked on a schools tour taking in thirty-four schools in Scotland and the North of England, and publicizing the shows through competitions in regional newspapers. Pupils at the schools had to give a reason why they thought the band should play at their school, and send it to their local paper. But the reaction far exceeded Lee's expectations.

'Originally, we had only planned to do one week of touring – a total of ten schools. But the response was huge and rather than disappoint we decided to make the schools tour last three weeks so we could visit more fans.'

'The response was truly amazing,' remembers Lee. 'At one school, the kids were going mental and even the schoolteachers were standing on chairs screaming and yelling for us to do an encore. It was fantastic. Afterwards, two roadies had to disguise themselves as members of 911 to try to distract the fans who had surrounded our car whilst we were getting changed in a classroom. But it didn't work. Eventually, though I still don't know how, we managed to escape alive. There were rude lipstick messages all over the car and notes attached to the windscreen wipers.'

But the adventures didn't end there. Another memorable occasion was on a trip from Wick in the North of Scotland to Inverness. Spike remembers this fateful journey only too well.

RAY BURMISTON

'It was about midnight and we were heading towards Inverness. There were five of us travelling together in the tour van and we were all extremely cold and desperate to go to our beds. As we were driving along this quiet road, something fell off the end of the van. At the time we thought nothing of it but a few minutes later the van started to lose speed until it eventually stopped dead in the middle of a field.'

'We thought that our tour guy was having a laugh with us,' continues Jimmy, 'but it turned out that we had genuinely broken down. We were in the middle of nowhere with absolutely no phone box in sight. By luck someone managed to get a reception on their mobile phone and called the AA. It was so cold out there but eventually, after the longest two hours of my life, the AA van arrived.

'There was nothing he could do to get the van working,' explains Lee, 'so he offered to take us to Inverness in his van. Now that seemed like a good idea but this van was so small that it would probably only seat two people comfortably at the best of times, and there were five of us. We didn't care, we just piled in. Who says life on the road is glamorous?'

The schools tour was hugely successful and boosted the band's following several fold, just in time for their début single release.

'Night to Remember' was released on 29 April 1996 and did far better than anyone had expected, thanks largely to the schools tours, limited radio play and one or two regional TV slots.

The following Saturday, 911 were performing at a show at Glasgow's Mitchell Theatre when the news came through that they had entered the Scottish Top Twenty. That night, the boys were performing a medley of three songs – Wet Wet Wet's 'Goodnight Girl', Kool & The Gang's 'Cherish', and a Take That track.

The following day, the trio drove south for a road-show in Crewe, and nervously waited to hear if their popularity in Scotland would show in the British Top Forty run-down. Near Chelmsford, the team pulled into a lay-by to take an advance call that was suggesting their single may have made the Top Forty. Excited, they tuned into the radio to listen to Mark Goodier announcing the charts for that week, and heard it confirmed that they had made it to number thirty-eight. Everyone was taken by surprise.

'We had hoped for the top seventy-five, but this was amazing,' says Jimmy. 'We just couldn't believe it.'

Another celebration ensued, this time with the lads enjoying a slap-up meal at a nearby Little Chef! Jimmy feasted on a salad, Lee munched on a chicken burger and Spike tucked into a burger, chips and baked beans.

'I have to eat baked beans with everything,' explains Spike. 'I eat at least three tins a day. When we go to posh hotels and everyone else is asking for roast beef, I always ask for baked beans! I like beans, toast and grated cheese, but my favourite is chips, eggs and beans. I love 'em and don't have any problems with wind. Beans give me energy for dancing.'

Jimmy, who has the healthiest eating habits in 911, adds: 'I don't think "Night To Remember" charting hit me until about a week later. When we heard we were number thirty-eight, we all ran around the Little Chef car park. We looked very strange, but didn't care because we were so pleased. Unlike the others,' he added, 'I don't eat junk food. I'm not into chocolate and crisps. The lads take the mick out of me 'cos all I ever eat is salad and fruit

'Some of us were crying,' recalls Lee of their Little Chef episode. 'It was very emotional. We had hoped the single would get into the Top Seventy-Five to get the buzz going. If I'd known, when I joined the band, it would take a year for us to release our first single, I'd have thought: Naaah, I can't wait that long. But, when we got together, we gave ourselves about two months to try and get things right. And this was the right way to do it.'

If Backlash had expected to turn up the following morning to find the phones red hot with A&R men eager to sign up the latest sensations who had charted without any of the muscle of the majors behind them, they were disappointed. The industry thought it was a fluke, a one off.

But there was no stopping 911 now, they had a clear vision of what they had to do.

'What we do now is release another record,' said Jimmy. 'We did it once, so we can do it again.'

# 'love sensation'

The second single was an easy choice. Since Glaswegian John McLaughlin had penned the song 'Love Sensation' in a day and presented it to the group, it had been a firm favourite with Spike, Lee and Jimmy, and soon after with the fans.

Once again, Eliot Kennedy was there to produce the song, backed up by a promotion video. Filmed over two days in the Spanish resort of Malgaluf and directed by Steve Price, the video was featured on *The Chart Show* in advance of the single's release. Two CD versions of 'Love Sensation', backed with an early version of 'Bodyshakin'', then came out in July.

In Sheffield, the boys left a Hallam FM roadshow where they had been performing alongside The Spice Girls, Sean McGuire and Peter Andre, feeling apprehensive about the chart run-down to come.

'As we finished the show, we all felt nervous about the charts,' recalls Lee. 'We gathered together in a car park to listen to the radio. Then, at about 6 p.m., came the news. We were absolutely delighted and more than a bit excited. I still can't believe it. We immediately called our family and friends to share the good news.'

The record had charted at number twenty-one, kept from the last Top Twenty place by Spike and Jimmy's musical heroes New Edition with their come-back single 'Hit Me Off'.

Jimmy was stunned when he heard the good news. 'I just couldn't believe it,' he says. 'I went tingly all over.'

The phones hadn't rung when 'Night To Remember' peaked at number thirty-eight. But, this time, the phones in the new offices on the south bank of Glasgow's River Clyde were red hot. Everybody wanted a part of 911.

Record companies, keen to buy up the rights to release the single around the world, called the Glasgow office asking to be put through to the international department. These were the first indications that 911's international career was about to take off.

'Could they be signed?' asked one caller.

'How much do they want?' demanded another.

'Who the hell are 911 anyway?' groaned an irate A&R man from Germany, no doubt reprimanded by his director for missing out on Britain's hottest new pop band.

Little did the majors in the UK, or elsewhere for that matter, know that the five-strong team of people who had piloted 911's career were crammed into a tiny two-room office in Glasgow's Clydeside and had achieved their chart success on a shoestring budget.

The band had to be resourceful when it came to staying within their tour budget. In order to cut costs, while performing roadshows far and wide, 911 were sleeping four to a room in Travelodges around the UK.

'We could only afford one room at £40 a night, so we all piled in. Our budget for food each day was a whopping £3.99 per person, so we'd end up eating things like fried egg sandwiches, with Spike always getting chips, beans and egg. Perhaps that's why he still loves this food so much. At one Travelodge, we had difficulty sneaking Spike in because the manageress had guessed what we were up to. To get him in, we had to open the window to our room, which would only budge about six inches. There we were trying to smuggle Spike in through the window when he got stuck and the manageress walked in. We were well caught!'

911's producer Eliot Kennedy spent the summer working with other pop acts including Kavana and The Spice Girls along with 911. No sooner had The Spice Girls vacated their rooms at the Kennedy studios than 911 arrived and dumped their bags on the bedroom floors. Their arrival heralded the beginning of work on their début album.

Meantime the band built a steady fan base. 911 never took their fans for granted.

'I save all my fan-mail so I can reply to as much of it as possible,' says Lee. 'We get loads of mad letters from girls who want to have our babies.'

But not all fans are content just to write to the group or get a glimpse of the boys at their shows.

'The fans have a system and seem to know everything,' says Jimmy. 'One fan will go to one place and another will go to a different area in the city until they have all the different areas covered. They'll contact each other on mobile phones. It's a very sophisticated process. They tend to cruise around the streets until they find us. We even had a taxi driver who switched off his lights late one night when he was following us. We were trying to lose him and that way we wouldn't see him so easily – very clever. I'm telling you, our fans would make great detectives.'

'Fans call us up through the night when we are sleeping,' adds Spike, 'and ask things like: "Are you awake?" They also knock on the doors – all because someone in the hotel wants to look smart and tells them what room we are in.'

By now record labels were desperate to get their hands on the hottest unsigned pop sensations by a mile. And, for the next few months, 911 were in the enviable position of choosing which record label they wanted to sign up with. But the key to their continued success was not to wait for a record deal. Instead the drive and determination which had launched 911's career and had piloted them successfully higher up the charts since the release of their début single some six months before, prompted 911 and their team to press ahead with their planned third single 'Don't Make Me Wait'.

# 'don't make me wait'

The group's style and sound was maturing after 'Love Sensation', which had been a summer pop tune. The third single had to be special.

Attention was paid to the song's introduction – a complex string arrangement that helped launch the song to radio disc jockeys. David Grant, formerly of the 80s band Lynx and Take That's vocal coach, was enlisted to help the guys to continue to improve their voices as the hits piled up.

The video for the single was shot at a steam railway station in Buckfastleigh, South Devon, and proved more sophisticated than the usual promo videos for most pop groups.

The band had travelled overnight from Aberdeen to Devon, arriving at 5.30 a.m., just in time for the shoot. Director Steve Price chose a model, called Maria, from Amsterdam, to be the focus of the boys' attention in a storyline which centred around Lee, Jimmy and Spike trying to get her to notice them. This was another first for 911 – they had to act.

'We had a great laugh doing the video and it was a really peaceful location with an excellent river nearby,' said Spike. 'I just wish I'd taken my fishing rod! We even got to use our very own steam engine which we were told was one of the trains that Queen Victoria had travelled in and, by coincidence, was called King George 911 – fate or what! It was our very first acting video, but I don't think Hollywood was that impressed because they haven't phoned. Brad Pitt has nothing to worry about.'

'There was one scene in the video,' Jimmy added, 'where 500 gallons of freezing cold water was poured over us. Believe me it was as cold as it looked.'

This was particularly unfortunate for Spike who, soaked through and wearing thick denims, had a hundred-yard walk back to his trailer.

'Try doing that with no underpants on,' he winces. 'I thought it was a clever way of getting out of my wet clothes quickly, but I could hardly move because my denims had become so heavy. Cold is not the word. I just wish I'd worn my winter woollies.'

'The water became so cold I could hardly breathe at one point,' Lee added. 'We weren't wearing shoes or socks when we filmed the water scene. It was freezing.'

The cold was worth it – the video for 'Don't Make Me Wait' was sensational. Unfortunately, not long after director Steve shouted 'Cut!' an unexpected incident happened. Emergency Services had to be called when a backflip Spike had attempted went wrong as he plummeted off the stage at a *Mizz* roadshow at Birmingham's NEC, during a performance of 'Don't Make Me Wait'. He sustained torn ligaments and tendons to his right ankle.

The accident, just three weeks before the group were due to release their third single, left him hobbling around on crutches for six weeks. His timing couldn't have been worse.

'I fell 6ft off the stage and thought I'd broken my ankle,' Spike recalls. 'I climbed back on in severe pain, and whispered to Lee that I thought I'd hurt my ankle. He thought I was having a laugh with him and just said,

"Shut up and get on with it. We've still got two songs to go." After the performance I had to limp off. It was just a bad sprain, but it put me out of action for a bit. Now I find the whole incident a little bit embarrassing and very amusing.'

The boys were feeling increasingly positive about the way things were going for them. Spike continued performing, despite his injury. His group-mates Lee and Jimmy helped to relieve his frustration while the intensive promotional work continued throughout the six weeks that Spike had to endure getting around on crutches.

'The guys were great,' Spike reveals. 'They wheeled me around on airport trolleys and helped to make my injuries more bearable. It was the most exciting time of our lives. Getting used to the crutches was a real nightmare at first, but I became really good with them and started whacking everyone with them whenever they annoyed me.'

With the release of 'Don't Make Me Wait' forthcoming, a second schools tour beckoned. This time the tour would visit schools in England and would feature Spike on crutches! As with their first tour, hysteria broke out with teachers having to hold back hysterical fans. At one school just outside London, security had to be drafted in to free the band when delighted pupils surrounded the school premises refusing to let their idols leave. Never before had the teachers seen such hysteria.

Later that week, pop supremo Jonathan King called 911 to say he thought that 'Don't Make Me Wait' was the best song he'd heard in ten years. And, for the first time ever, King put the song on the cover of his industry insider magazine, *The Tip Sheet*, which tracks new releases and predicts the rise of new talent, on two consecutive weeks.

As promotion for the new single ensued Virgin Records became increasingly impressed by the achievement of 911 and their team. Paul Conroy, Managing Director of the company, was aware that 911 had built a brilliant team behind them, including their personal manager Steve, business manager Frank, PR and press expert Julie, fanclub supremo Martin, production manager Stuart, producer Eliot, a strong team of songwriters, and the band's former plugger Neil Ferris – later to become Managing Director of EMI Records.

Conroy asked his staff how it could be that a band, such as 911, could enter the charts on a shoestring budget while many major labels were struggling to get the public's attention for their new pop acts. With Virgin Records already the home of The Spice Girls and George Michael, Paul Conroy was also only too aware that 911's pop band was creating a sensation wherever it appeared in the UK.

It was decided that a production deal between Virgin Records and the Ginga Recording Company would best serve 911. The band and their team were flown to the label's London headquarters to sign the deal on Lee's 21st birthday, 27 September 1996.

It was planned that on this significant day 911 would

perform an exclusive set of songs for their new record company, but Spike's injury put an end to such an idea. Instead, in the massive conference room at Virgin Record's Kensal House building, 911's pop videos were screened to *Live & Kicking* producer Cathy Gilby, a host of teen magazine editors, 911 and Virgin lawyers. Also present were key people from within the company – including top brass at the label, Paul Conroy and Ray Cooper, and the Ginga/Backlash team who had so impressed Virgin.

After the deal was signed that afternoon, Paul Conroy gave a speech welcoming the band and the Backlash team to the Virgin family. He said, 'We want to make 911 massive all around the world. For 911's management team to come out of Glasgow and do what they have on a shoestring is amazing.'

Frank Shapiro had no illusions about the potential of the contract and immediately began planning for the future. 'Everyone thinks when you sign a huge deal that the money comes in all at once,' he explained. 'That's not the case. The cash is strategically planned for the future, otherwise the guys would be flying around in helicopters and wearing Armani suits. We'll make sure they have a decent life and don't blow their money.'

After the celebrations were over, the band flew back to Glasgow.

On the Monday, Jimmy, Lee and Spike and the Backlash team all received bottles of Champagne from Virgin with the message, 'Welcome to the Virgin family'.

As soon as the deal was clinched Lee's spirits were lifted immeasurably. 'Throughout 1996,' he said, 'we did most things on our own. Then we got signed up and it has been non-stop hard work ever since. So that was a big break for us.'

He told his friends in Carlisle: 'Things are looking good. We're getting a great reaction at all the road-shows. When they used to announce 911, everyone would go, "Who?" Now people are getting to know who we are. I've spent years fantasizing about something like this. It's a dream come true.'

It was a new beginning.

'Paul Conroy is the man who deals with Meatloaf on a daily basis and he's now dealing with 911,' laughs Jimmy. 'I just hope we aren't as huge as him – not physically, you understand!'

The press quickly woke up to the news of this significant signing. Stories started to appear about how much the deal was worth and it seemed that with every story a couple of million pounds were added on to the last figure reported. The 911 lads saw this as an opportunity to have a laugh with the press.

'We told one newspaper that we had asked for Pot Noodles as part of our record deal' Lee explained, 'because that's what we survived on in the early days when we had no money and it was only fair we shouldn't forget where we came from. They believed me! I'd rather eat them than a bag of chips. I've tried chicken and sweetcorn, beef and tomato, but chicken and mushroom is definitely the one for me! They're dead easy to make, and they fill you up between meals – I love 'em.'

With the might of Virgin behind them, 'Don't Make Me Wait' was released on 28 October, helped along by unprecedented TV coverage including *Blue Peter*, *Newsround*, *The O-Zone*, *The Chart Show*, *The*

*Disney Club* and Richard and Judy's *This Morning* appearances.

'I love everything about "Don't Make Me Wait",' said Lee. 'It's a dead sing-along song and I like the violin start to it.'

During the week of release, 911 played a show in Bangor, Northern Ireland. 'The gig in Bangor was funny,' laughs Stuart Owen. 'An ashtray and a full bottle of Newcastle Brown were thrown at the band. It was quite sad, really. We had to get out of there in a hurry. Even so, the car was covered in lipstick.'

After a gruelling day of promotion, 911 headed back to their hotel. Out of the car window, Lee, Spike and Jimmy stared in disbelief at uniformed officers pointing machine guns at them.

'We were stopped at a border checkpoint,' Jimmy explains. 'Our car had been trashed after a gig by people writing rude messages on it with lipstick and we definitely looked a bit suspicious. They pulled us over and two guys with machine guns made me get out and open the boot.'

The officers asked Jimmy to open the metallic suitcases which filled the car boot.

'What's in the case?' asked the officer in charge.

'It's only microphones, honest,' Jimmy told him, opening the cases to reveal the truth.

Before long Spike, Lee and Jimmy were signing autographs for the officers and laughing at the misunderstanding. Lee, Spike and Jimmy were performing at a roadshow in Northampton when they heard that 'Don't Make Me Wait' had provided them with their first taste of top ten success.

'We were over the moon and were travelling back to the hotel to have a quiet celebration, but it wasn't to be,'

says Spike. 'You see, when we got to our hotel in London there was a big surprise waiting for us – our mums! They had travelled all the way down to spend the evening with us and celebrate our success. We were dead chuffed to see them again and it was a complete shock to us.'

The radio-friendly single shot straight into the Top Ten at number ten and provided 911 with their first appearance on *Top of the Pops*. Again they broke the mould for a pop band's début stint on the show. Ric Blaxill, *Top of the Pops'* producer at the time, had assumed the group would mime and was impressed when Lee told him he would sing live. As the band prepared for their first appearance on 8 November 1996, nerves got the better of them.

'We thought we'd be perfectly relaxed,' recalled Spike, 'but we kept having to go to the toilet. Once we'd performed and finished rehearsals and recording, though, we had a right laugh. We thought Lee was getting a bit big-headed, so we made him walk around with a traffic cone on his head. Most people would have felt a prat, but Lee took it in his stride.'

'Our television début on *Top of the Pops* was amazing,' Jimmy said. 'We were quite surprised at how small the studio was and how the various pop stars were just walking about. We passed Simply Red in the corridor which was very odd.'

'The first *Top of the Pops* was something they'd always wanted to do and they'll always remember that,' says press manager Julie. 'They were very nervous and panicking about their performance which, as always, was brilliant. Lee always sings live and was very good that day.'

Also on the programme were Blackstreet and Ocean Colour Scene. But if 911 were nervous, their presence on *Top of the Pops* helped relax another pop hopeful – Moby.

As Ric Blaxill revealed: 'I was surprised to learn that Moby was really excited about being on the same show as pop lads 911. It turned out that he is really superstitious and took it as a good omen that 911 were on the programme – his birthday is on the 9th of the 11th. And, to think, I thought he was a big fan of the band!'

# 'the day we find love'

As Christmas 1996 approached, 911 gave one of their best appearances at George Square, Glasgow – the city they now collectively called their second home.

Glasgow's Shine On Festival 1996 was a Christmas extravaganza featuring a host of pop acts. But the fans had only one thing on their minds. Dozens tried to storm the security cordon to get close to Spike, Lee and Jimmy who were warming up backstage. And by the time the lads had sung four songs, including a first-ever performance of 'The Day We Find Love', planned as the band's first 1997 single, screaming fans proved that 911 were no hype.

The trio had agreed to headline the event as the city's Christmas lights were switched on, but caused a security scare when their fans laid siege to their nearby hotel afterwards – trapping the group in the building. Outside, in the bitter winter cold, hundreds of girls attempted to storm the Copthorne Hotel, just yards from the George Square stage.

'We couldn't believe it. It was total pandemonium,' said Lee. 'We wanted to go outside and meet the fans, but were told by the police to stay inside and keep away from the windows in case they started a riot.'

'It was funny really,' Spike said. 'The police even threatened to charge us with intent to cause a riot!'

'We just couldn't get out of our hotel,' Jimmy explained. 'There were over 4000 fans there. We were stuck. We suddenly discovered that in Glasgow fans are so dedicated to you that they'll stand outside your hotel room for five or six hours. Everywhere you go, they're there supporting you.'

For the trio, it was a sign of things to come. A few days after the George Square concert, 911 were asked to take part in the *Smash Hits* 1996 roadshow, due to kick off later that month. Ironically, only twelve months earlier they had had to beg for the chance to open the *Smash Hits* tour in Glasgow with just one song. Now they were being asked to headline. 911 appeared at the opening date of the *Smash Hits* Tour '96 at Manchester's G-Mex, with fourteen other pop acts, among them Mark Morrison and Boyzone.

The show proved to be a home-coming event for Spike. The 5ft-4in (and a half!) heart-throb from nearby Warrington, admits: 'Playing Manchester was – and still is – really important to me. It's like getting the stamp of approval from all the people who know me.'

Each night, for over three hours, the performing artists worked their magic on the fans, but few of the performers can have been as satisfied as Jimmy. A deafening scream filled the cavernous SECC hall in Glasgow each time compere, Tristan Bancks, mentioned that 911 were lined up to close the *Smash Hits* show.

As they completed the tour, Jimmy breathed a sigh of relief.

'The reception we got was unbelievable,' he told his Aunt Trish. 'Now we can look back over the past twelve months and say all the hard work has really paid off. I know we've had our critics, but we seemed to have silenced them and are getting ready for our début album in the New Year. 1997's going to be a good year for 911.'

Next on the agenda was the illustrious *Smash Hits* Poll Winners' Party held at the famous London Docklands. Other artists performing on the day were East 17, Boyzone and Robbie Williams. 911 were stunned when they learned that they had been nominated for a number of important awards including Best New Act. They came second in the poll, kept only from the title by none other than The Spice Girls. The band's first *Smash Hits* front cover, just before Christmas, was another high point for the group.

The international promotions began directly after the release of 'Don't Make Me Wait' when the band visited most European countries. While, in the UK, 911 were fast becoming a household name, the trio had to start afresh abroad.

In the first month of the international promotions, they were whisked to Spain, France, Germany, Switzerland, Norway and Austria. Each member of 911 has their favourite experience of Europe.

'I enjoyed visiting Spain,' says Jimmy. 'They really seemed to like our music and hopefully, there'll be loads more visits. It's a really lovely place and the people are really friendly.'

For Lee, Norway stood out.

'It was really beautiful,' he said. 'The place looks really cool.'

'Yeah. Me, too,' adds Spike. 'I really liked Norway because it's full of big lakes with people fishing on them, and everybody knows how much I love fishing.'

In Switzerland, travelling with GMTV for a special broadcast, the boys got their first opportunity to snowboard.

'Before the cameras began rolling the boys were practising snowboarding,' recalled one GMTV exec. 'Lee was hopeless. Spike wasn't too bad and Jimmy was snowboarding like a true professional. However, as soon as the cameras were turned on, Jimmy fell on his backside. He was so disappointed because no-one would now believe he could snowboard.'

By now the band's European promo tours were beginning to pay dividends. Television stations, journalists and, most important of all, the fans in Europe were keen to get another chance to see the band. But the boys knew that, to keep the momentum going and make sure that they weren't going to be another flash in the pan, they had to better their previous efforts in Britain. They released 'The Day We Find Love' as their fourth single on 10 February 1997.

'I love it 'cos it's a top track written by Eliot Kennedy,' Jimmy says. 'I mean the guy's a genius. He's responsible for The Spice Girls' song "Say You'll Be There" and Take That's "Everything Changes". Need I say more?'

'Keep your fingers crossed that it will be our biggest hit to date,' Lee told his mum as they released 'The Day We Find Love'.

'We knew we couldn't sit back and say we were where we wanted to be yet,' he recalls. 'Our first single "Night To Remember" went into the Top Forty, then "Love Sensation" got to twenty-one, and our third single "Don't Make Me Wait" sold over 100,000 copies. It also cracked the Top Ten. But with each success came a fresh challenge – namely to improve on our previous hit.'

Emotional scenes surrounded the chart run-down for the band's fourth single, their second with Virgin Records. Die-hard fans had tracked Lee, Jimmy and Spike to Glasgow's Hilton Hotel where the lads were enjoying a rare weekend off. As they were joined by a close circle of friends, their management team and family members, Jimmy sipped a Jack Daniels and Coke while Spike and Lee downed lagers. Then, as the hour approached for Radio 1's Mark Goodier to announce that week's Top Ten, they went in search of a room with a radio.

'The rooms' radios weren't working,' recalls Spike. 'So we had to give up and go outside to listen in our business manager, Frank's car. We opened all the car doors and sun-roof and everybody piled in. Lee, Jimmy and I were outside with about fifty fans who'd surrounded the car.'

When 911 were announced as that week's number ten, fans broke down in tears as they hugged their idols. Some were crying because they feared 911 would now become too big for them to follow their career closely.

Lee comforted one teenage girl, 'Don't worry, we will always be there for our fans. We chose to spend our weekend off with you all and we know that without you we could never have made it into the Top Ten.'

There was no time for Lee, Spike and Jimmy to sit

back and bask in the glory of their biggest hit so far. By this time, they had almost completed recording their début album, produced by Eliot Kennedy and his partners Tim Lever and Mike Percy.

They even got the chance to go to the famous Abbey Road Studios as the finishing touches were put on the LP.

'It was cool,' said Spike, 'thinking that we were standing in the very same studio where The Beatles had recorded their music.'

Just eight days after the 'Day We Find Love' single charted, 911's début album 'The Journey' was released. The trio knew the importance of their first LP and decided to take themselves to the fans with a series of in-store signings at record stores throughout the UK. After each day's signing, tour manager John Pryer had to remove the teddy bears and cuddly toys from the tour van. There were so many gifts that his hotel room was a mountain of presents from fans.

Back in Glasgow, where they hadn't signed records since that summer's release of 'Love Sensation', in excess of 5000 fans turned up at HMV's Argyle Street store for what was supposed to be a thirty-minute session signing 'The Journey' album. But, such was the demand, the signing session in front of tearful fans lasted over three hours.

'Some fans asked for various parts of their anatomy to be signed,' recalls Jimmy. 'Of course, we declined because we're all gentlemen. Or, at least, that's the official story!'

As a police escort rescued the lads from hysterical fans, some stores decided that the sheer popularity of the band had reached an unprecedented scale and advised the group to cancel their visit for safety reasons.

'We had mixed emotions about cancelling some signings,' says PR manager Julie MacCaskill. 'But 911 have always prided themselves on the fact that the safety of their fans comes first. Even if one fan had been injured it would have been one fan too many. It was a tough

MIKE PRIOR, IDOLS

choice to make, but it was the right one and, I suppose, it was an enviable dilemma to be in.'

In Liverpool, Jimmy's hometown, a signing went ahead in the Virgin store at Clayton Square's pedestrianized shopping centre despite the band losing their way. By the time they arrived, over 3000 fans were packed into the square, many pressed against the shop's windows and chanting 911's songs. As the doors opened, a surge of over-excited fans splurged into the shop. The police had to stop the signings after just fifteen minutes.

'We were gutted,' said Spike. 'Again, we were just too popular for our own good.'

That same week, the boys got another taste of pop history in the making by going along to the Brit Awards alongside top music legends, such as Elton John, The Bee Gees and George Michael.

Mark Morrison, who had just performed a stunning version of 'Return Of The Mack' with scantily-clad mock policewomen, strolled up to Jimmy. 'Hey, Jimmy from 911. I love your music,' he told him.

This really was the life.

Despite the album's release coinciding with The Brits, which is known to increase the sales of nominated major acts by as much as a hundred per cent, 'The Journey' still managed an impressive chart position of thirteen.

# 'bodyshakin''

A week later, the trio were shooting the video for 'Bodyshakin''. An early version of the song had started life as a B-side on the band's second single and hadn't been thought of as a potential single. But the reaction of the fans to the song outstripped all expectations. The song was a favourite of Spike's because it had a great dance routine, and he had impressed Lee and Jimmy with his enthusiasm for it.

'I think we should do a really funky, full-on version of "Bodyshakin'",' he told them. 'It's one of the songs we love. The fans really like it, too, and it's great to perform even if Lee can't bodyshake to save himself!'

Jimmy agreed: 'I just love "Bodyshakin'". It's exactly my kind of music.'

When Lee heard the plan he agreed. 'The song has become an anthem to our fans. I really like performing it on stage because it's got a cool dance routine. Even if I can't bodyshake!'

Because the song was performance-led, 911 decided to make a performance video at London's Forum in Kentish Town, involving a select audience of 200 fan club members.

Behind closed doors, the band filmed from 8.30 a.m., to 10 p.m., and performed 'Bodyshakin'' to cameras twenty times. Exhausted, they then let the doors be opened to the lucky audience and soon forgot all about their fatigue. They went on to perform the routine, backed by a live band who had worked with Take That and East 17, yet another twenty times in front of the live crowd.

Remarkably, as the director shouted 'Cut', 911 immediately performed an exclusive set of album tracks as a bonus for the excited extras.

Throughout the day, Spike had noticed one special girl waving to him. Little Colette Baxter, just five, was pulled on stage by Spike who sang 'Our Last Goodbye' to her.

'Spike is her favourite,' Colette's mum recalls. 'She'd been waving to him throughout the show and he asked her up on to the stage. She's made another friend now.'

The 'Bodyshakin'' release, on 21 April 1997, meant the band were asked to appear on another string of top TV programmes. This included *Top of the Pops* which provided one of the band's most memorable live performances, featuring a spectacular pyrotechnic display.

As the boys waited for their turn to record 'Bodyshakin'' for *Top of the Pops*, they bumped into ex Take That star, Robbie Williams, and challenged him to a game of football.

'He was a cracking laugh and we had a good chat about what you get up to on the road,' Spike reveals. 'He knows some people from my hometown Warrington so we talked about them. He was a really nice lad. We just had a kick-around, but if we'd played him for real we'd have beaten him, no sweat.'

A couple of days later, at *Noel's House Party*, Spike Lee and Jimmy – pretending they were decorators out to spruce up the House – met their idols The Bee Gees. Later, Maurice, Robin and Barry told Capital Radio they were impressed by the boys' performance and Lee's vocals. Lee, the legendary trio told the radio station, was one of the best singers they had heard in years.

'Bodyshakin'' débuted at number three, behind chart-topper R Kelly with I 'Believe I Can Fly', and Michael Jackson at number two.

Spike attributes their phenomenal success to the fact that 911 had widened their appeal. 'Lads round our way liked the song,' he said. 'They loved it because it's a good song to dance to.'

For the first time, the guys were apart as a single charted. Spike was spending time with family and friends in Warrington. Jimmy and Lee had hoped to be in Glasgow that Sunday to spend the chart run-down with the Backlash team. But, as they were collected from the airport by Frank and production co-ordinator Stuart, the announcement that they were number three blared out from the car stereo.

Delighted, Jimmy couldn't hold his excitement. He rolled down the car window as they barrelled along the M8 and yelled out to other bemused drivers: 'We're number THREE! We're number THREE! That's us on the radio.'

That night Lee, Jimmy, Steve, Frank, Julie, Martin, Stuart and accountant Stuart Overend enjoyed an Indian meal at Glasgow's newly-opened Kama Sutra.

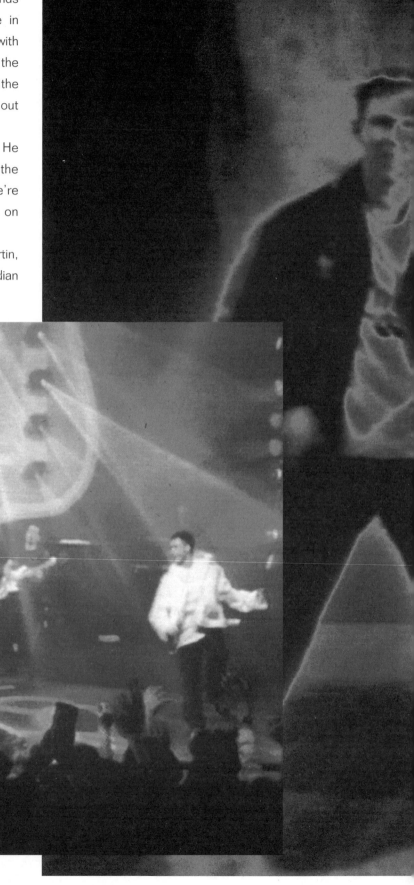

# taking on the world

The boys' passports were soon full of even more exotic stamps. Their first trip to South East Asia in May 1997 was phenomenal, they were treated like royalty. In Malaysia, they performed at massive shopping centres which were closed down each day for the show. Masses of children hung from the shopping centre balconies. The band were number one in Malaysia before they'd even set foot in the country and have subsequently gone five times platinum there. 'The Journey' spent over three months at number one in the album charts, outselling Bon Jovi, and Michael Jackson.

'We're bigger in South East Asia than we are here,' admits Lee who is astonished by the success there. 'The fans are absolutely mental out there, though polite at the same time. I can't actually believe it because we're bigger than The Spice Girls in Malaysia, which is odd considering they're absolutely massive in the UK.'

'We've made a lot of friends over there,' adds Jimmy, 'so it'll be nice to go back.'

Spike agrees: 'The people had a very funny sense of humour over there and we had a really great laugh with them all. We went jet-skiing and stuff. Now I want to buy my own jet-ski.'

The boys had to adapt to each country's laws and customs, particularly in Singapore where it is illegal to chew or import gum. Chewing gum was banned in 1992 because it causes a mess.

In June 1997, the band enjoyed their first holiday in six months. It may not sound much, but they hadn't had a day off during that spell. They had been so busy promoting the album, singles and doing international promotions, that there had been no time for leisure. Now they had ten days to do whatever they wanted.

Getting away from it all, Jimmy went to Henlow Grange Health Farm in Bedfordshire.

'I spent three days being pampered with lots of healthy things like aromatherapy and reflexology. It was great and it was the perfect wind-down to what had been a hectic promotional schedule.'

Lee, on the other hand, went to Menorca with song-writer John.

'We just chilled out and wrote songs,' Lee remembers. 'We went to a quiet fishing village and I thought that I'd get away from it all for a while. But, on the second day there, I got spotted. By the end of the day, there were thirty or forty people outside my hotel room singing 911 songs for me. On one occasion when I was in the shower getting ready, all I could hear was this group of people outside my balcony singing, "You got my bodyshakin'". They knew all the words which was quite cool.'

While there, Lee and John met 'The Golden Girls', but they weren't the famous American comedy trio or, for that matter, a romantic interest. They were five widows from Ireland and, by the end of their holiday trip, they were 911 fans.

'We met them on the last day of our holiday,' Lee said. 'They were absolutely mental and fun.'

Spike went to Gran Canaria with his brother, Mike, and some friends.

'I went sharkfishing one day,' says Spike, 'which was strange because I'm scared of sharks. But it was fun. I was seasick, though, and had to throw up over the side of the boat which was nice for all my mates, I don't think.'

Soon 911's American label was making plans to release the band to a US audience in the wake of the British pop invasion. In July, the band spent three weeks on the Elite models tour, visiting sixty radio stations, being interviewed by journalists and meeting key industry movers and shakers. Flying from state to state, they travelled to Los Angeles, San Francisco, New York, Orlando, Miami, Dallas, Houston, New Jersey, Providence, Boston and Chicago. Although they were nowhere near as well received as they had been in South East Asia, US radio stations responded well to the group.

Lee, Jimmy and Spike started each day at 7 a.m., and carried on until 10 p.m.

'America is such a big place and things are just starting to break there,' says Lee. 'We're keeping our fingers crossed. The Spice Girls have just cracked the pop market there so, hopefully, they've opened the door for the 911 invasion.'

Averaging four-to-five hours sleep each night, they were exhausted but high on the prospect of their impending American success.

'Love Sensation' quickly became a favourite among the US record label chiefs who thought the track perfect as a theme song for the *Casper 2* soundtrack, the follow-up to the hugely successful *Casper The Friendly Ghost* feature film. A few calls later, the song had been confirmed as the theme song on the video release, in October 1997.

'It's such a big film, I thought at first they were winding us up when they said they wanted us,' said Spike.

Just as important, 'Love Sensation' was chosen as the first single release in America.

In August, the band flew to Korea for a week before going on to Taiwan where they played to a crowd of 15,000 and braved Typhoon Winnie.

When the band drove to the Grand Hyatt Hotel in the capital Taipei, scenes of devastation were already in evidence as blocks of flats collapsed in the storm. Trees had been uprooted, cars overturned and a state of emergency announced.

Over three days, the freak weather conditions terrified people in Taiwan.

'It was really frightening,' says Spike. 'We were all in our hotel when suddenly this tree flew past our window.'

Yet the band still made the most of their visit.

'We were there and had to get on with it,' admits Lee. 'We still went out and did photo-shoots and radio and TV visits. They had what they call a typhoon holiday where everything was cancelled. The typhoon was really bad, but we got out and travelled about in a van because we knew we wouldn't get another chance for some time. There was a lot of wreckage, very high winds and a lot of rain – just like British winters really!'

'We decided, "Hey, we come from the North of England. It rains there all the time. We'll go out and deal with it",' adds Spike. 'Nobody was particularly worried.'

Meanwhile, the choice of 'Love Sensation' as the first American single meant the band would have to record a new video for the song. They re-shot in June, a year to the day after the original video for the song had been filmed in Majorca. This time, the video was shot at a fun park in Brighton.

'We had to go on the rollercoaster about fifteen times,' Lee recalls, 'so you can imagine I felt quite sick afterwards.'

'The US "Love Sensation" video was a cracking laugh,' Spike said, 'but Lee got a bit sick on the rollercoaster. Lee and I had to do the scene in a rubber dinghy. I was steering and I spun it round and round until Lee felt sick!'

# 'the journey'

The final track to be released from the début album 'The Journey' was the title track that held a special place in the hearts of the band's fans. Released on 30 June, it was a song which documented Lee's battle against Hodgkin's Disease when he was young and also charted the journey the band had made over the previous two years.

Lee's childhood battle with the illness had left him bloated and nearly bald. He used to come home from school each day and lie on the couch, drained of energy and fall asleep. Mysterious nosebleeds and a lump on his neck told his mum, Una, that something was seriously wrong. He was just eight when Hodgkin's Disease was first diagnosed. As little Lee underwent months of painful chemotherapy, his hair fell out and his weight eventually plummeted to a near fatal two and a half stones. But, thanks to his belief that, one day, he would be famous, he fought his way back to health.

As well as the chemotherapy, which made Lee's hair fall out as a side-effect, he had to take eighteen pills a day. A series of operations followed. By the time he was just two and a half stone, he had to be pushed around in a wheelchair because he hadn't the strength to walk.

'I was concerned whether I would live through it but every day I told myself what I was going to do when I got better. Throughout, I felt that my life would be different and I was certain that I would be on telly when I got older. I had a feeling that everything was planned. My photograph was in the local paper because of my illness and I feel that that publicity led on to what I'm doing now.'

Spike recalls, '"The Journey" told of the obstacles Lee had to overcome in his battle against cancer as a child and how he found strength from despair. It also explained how, as a group we've been through a lot together since 911 started. It's not been an easy journey. It's been a lot of hard work for everyone concerned. But it's beginning to pay off.'

Lee adds, 'I think the song told people how I felt being so ill, how I've coped and how I've changed as a result of my illness. Live for the moment and what you have.'

'"The Journey" was a song of inspiration and hope, and concluded the first chapter of 911's journey to pop superstardom.

'The Journey had a big influence on me,' says Jimmy. 'Sometimes it's difficult to imagine some of the problems people have, but the important thing to remember is that, no matter how big your troubles are, there is hope.'

Filmed a month before the release, 'The Journey' video was shot in a disused RAF hanger in Bedfordshire. It was so cold that, every so often, the band had to take a break because their mouths were freezing up and they couldn't sing.

Taking shelter in a nearby Portacabin, the boys took time out to think of their future and the journey ahead. Spike cradled a hot cup of soup and said: 'I know there's a lot of hard work ahead which is slightly daunting. But with the support of our fans we'll make it, I'm sure. I also know that I'll probably get into trouble along the way somewhere. That you can be sure of.'

The boys have recorded their seventh single 'Party People... Friday Night' which marks another departure for Lee, Spike and Jimmy and proves that they are not going to stick with a successful formula. All three band members sing on the track and the song has been remixed by Jon Douglas, famed for his work with George Michael.

The video for the song has now been recorded in the Los Angeles district of Bel-Air and features the lads at a car wash.

'It was brilliant fun recording the video for the single,' says Jimmy, 'and a bit more comfortable than some of the other videos we've had to make. The weather was fantastic and the models were beautiful. The car wash was really cool and helped cool us down when it got too hot for us.'

As with each of their previous singles, the boys have surprised their fans yet again.

Lee is already looking ahead to the release of the next single, the first from their planned second album.

'Yes,' he says, 'we're focusing on the second album now and the Arena Tour we've scheduled for 1998.

I can't wait. I just want to thank all our fans for being so wonderful to us since 911 was formed.'

'We love the fans,' Spike agrees, 'and we're always having a laugh with them. They've been great to us and without them, we wouldn't be in the charts. Who knows where we'd be now?'

'Yes,' Jimmy added, 'a big thank you to all the 911 fans. Thanks for a great time. We've still got a long journey ahead of us. The journey has just begun!'